I0522036

the catastrophe of after: a short-stay diary
Copyright © 2023 Emily Kay MacGriff

Original Cover Art by Emily Kay MacGriff

The font used is Spectral
The cover fonts are Frank Ruhl Libre and Corbel

All rights reserved. No duplication or reuse of any selection is allowed without the express written consent of the publisher.

Gnashing Teeth Publishing
242 East Main Street
Norman AR 71960

Printed in the United States of America

ISBN 979-8-987569412

Non-Fiction: Poetry

Gnashing Teeth Publishing First Edition

praise for the catastrophe of after: a short-stay diary

Emily's work speaks with a directness to me , the images deepen as I read them, I feel their physical presence ... there are stories in these poems, tight , humane , compassionate for the moment she catches ...excellent work.

Beau O'Reilly, playwright, cofounder of Maestro
Subgum & the Whole and Curious Theatre Branch

Emily MacGriff's poems circle the globe, moving almost deliriously from life in the arctic to intimate scenes between a mother and a baby, teetering all the while on dangerous emotional precipices. Through these dizzying moves, they craft startling "shapes like sour passion / fruit or sunken garlic," as if attempting to find the right snack to maintain equilibrium, "to not upset the sea / and keep my nose above water.

Nathan Hoks, author of *Nests in Air* and
The Narrow Circle amongst others

Emily Kay MacGriff writes with precision; her lines stand alone. Each image is a complex repository of soul. In this work, Emily unlocks the taste of acorns and their mystery along with the bitterness of ashes and what frigid sea water feels like in the dark. An enjoyable, deep and enriching work of art. She engulfs the human form, highlighting the active contrasts of human nature, life and death, love and need.

Iliana Regan, author of *Burn the Place* and *Fieldwork*

the catastrophe of after: a short-stay diary

by Emily Kay MacGriff

for my husband and our sons

table of contents

she had no technique; it was all the truth

before I have this baby I need to tell you
I wrote that poem about a mother hypothetically,
not my Mom, specifically - they don't have the same voice
or hair although one may recognize the other in cursive script.
before I have this baby I need

to tell you I never wanted to be the beautiful girl,
the happy girl with a row of white teeth trained on the world.

I was drawn
to the tragic girl in the worn lace dressing robe,
a cigarette draped over the side of a deep green silk chaise,
heavy curtain closed over leaded windows and just a sliver of moon
slipping in. I wanted to be alone in a reasonable house
dangling the curlicue of a matte mint landline
around my finger, just sober enough to be
undetected just under the table enough
to be maudlin.

I wanted to have the tinted lips of leftover makeover forgotten over
    powdery skin
and a pill or two in a tiny limoge box at the dressing table, tiny pearls
    lacquered to the top.

not Marilyn or Judy or Joan,
maybe Cindy down the street in Cleveland,
or Sara in Boston sipping rusty breeze
blown off the ocean behind a long shipping lane -

I wore
a tailored tweed jacket with shoulders slightly pointed in my thirties
on the L listening to Count Basie as steam rose from the track
after each train went by and by, too fast
inside a plume of vapor
that no one cared to smell

of tobacco anymore i imagined
my epitaph

she was a waif and here
is her hotel diary
the letters alone
are gold dust.

reticulate

I woke up blood red wild
from a sclerotic dream, wooden
shiplap scandinavian over frozen sea
buckling like rutilated quartz at 1AM

I heard the first frost settling into large tooth
aspen leaves unfilled with late November
as I always remembered it in Michigan.

I fell out of quilts to feel the chill
light on my arm hairs

and the baby kicked

in naked anticipation of *always*,

always coming soon.

we planted winter months to produce
millions of red crabs marching in an annual migration,
trampling on Christmas Island

hundreds of sheep in Mongolia have been walking in a circle
for 10 days on camera 6 feet
of snow in western New York
yesterday while two thigh high boots
languished by a wire trash can on Sovill Avenue
in Cleveland, one without a heel
and people are dying

when you're in your early twenties, you acknowledge
the people you love will suffer and decay, sometimes
before you. and you move

ahead anyway, connecting
pruning
invading
each other's *must*

like a root vine through a drainage pipe. you adopt
a dog, you acknowledge
it will break
and
pass

away, hopefully not for a decade
at which point

it all feels constant.

but juvenile whale sharks are shifting
the range of an entire population

is dying,

even after you spend a morning in rusted tintinnabulation

of first flurry, agape

<200 pounds of pregnant
and mostly d e   c   a   y   yourself>

at the daft snow flailing
so dearly
in the Kroger parking lot. I realized

your love makes me want
to die.

and my husband told me
last night
the moon fell over onto its back

feet   in the air
       up

i want to stay up all night breaking
your heart with my eyes closed
like a live power line snapping
on the sidewalk in fervent jerks of *what to do,*
what to do when your arms are a mountain
range to climb into and my chin is split
in mouthing remember me
at midnight with stars
dripping off the end
of *i tried.*

canyon rain

I only left
my bathroom window cracked
to let fresh night in, so I was surprised
when I couldn't sleep. I was surprised
to smell the dew settling
around the blackbirds and starlings
only out back for a day or two

how much longer
will there be fall heat –
how much longer can I breathe
in sips of thin wind slipping
under the eaves, slow,
like your finger dripping off my chin
as you fall asleep
and I sneak away again,
and again, and again toward winter

how long can i work with the same words

mashed in shapes like sour passion

fruit or sunken garlic, their colors grown the same

in manipulation, laziness is a catchall

for detachment, disassociation's viable cousin in crimson

velvet stolen through the front gate

of a yacht club we'll never belong to,

but i'll keep strolling you

to look at the same boats

capsizing under my new mother

weight and mourn how

even you can't recognize

my eyes in photos from my twenties

burnt into the trees along our street.

i want this poem to sound small

beside piano and violin on a frozen beach,

the last basking shark in Greenland at the bottom of algae sea,

smoky violet light crawling down a Victorian alleyway

rapping on each window, light as a broken wave reaching

toward sand dune willow, seaside goldenrod, beach pea

and me covered in star ash wishing

i was on the bald side of the universe

whispering

against empty

a   i   r

tickled amber

artifacts in ice patches

what's it called, that moment
when an airplane nose pulls up
with wheels still

on the ground, before air
catches wing and Bernoulli
promises

we will rise?

what's that moment when we're still alive,
when the first few starlings leap and leave
the flock on newly fallen leaves —
who decides when a murmuration starts?

what's that moment when
you can return to South America
from Shag Rocks instead of continuing on
to approach Antarctica, where I'll always recover —

Smeerenburg,

I dream often about late season
when I'll be much braver
than I was before

and in a smaller sailing ship
instead of large hulled steel —

the bears are closer then,
all around my Zodiac even
and I'll only use poles
like I'm guiding in Russia,
stakes out

to resemble walrus tusks
and trusting

the hummock
emerging from blizzard
like dozens of umbels
that would've shed
from queen anne's lace

and I don't believe
there are so many more ice mummies out there
but if there were, I'd have found them

I feel like they could tell me
what happens
to artifacts in ice patches.

and the bar was called colander

I drank cold water off New Jersey with small bits of ice, bleeding
into the waves as I drunkenly crawled along the salt flat full
with 4 pills in each hand meeting at the dance
up the beach and looking across the floor
toward my Mom who hadn't noticed

I'd gone
20 years ago

watching the show, realizing the woman
on the beach collecting bones
that seemed to come from birds
next to a bowhead whale rib –

this is how we prove the unprovable

showering off and using the thin two blade
razor under the sink for stray chin hairs

being held on a pale dock washed in late, late

closing my eyes against all of the sweat
drying in cool snowflakes on tangled skin,
warm in how it read your body backwards

and the bar was called colander,
as I recall it now, the next morning
leading with my heels.

checking in with labor

10 months pregnant in scuffed clogs and mismatched socks
spilling over the arches in swollen *we're alone*,
I saw a couple waiting
for their referral card.

her belly was small and he had long arms, a mask guard
they nuzzled like albatross at the reception desk, comforting
each other against whatever the card might fix, or might not.

if I had a kid in a wheelchair,
he said, I would not buy the remote
control wheelchair toy for my kid,
they'd want a regular car
and if I was a kid I would laugh at you or if I was a kid
and I had that I would cry
and go home.

she leaned her forehead against his bucket hat,
closed her eyes, tapped his shoulder
with a rolled up magazine.

I wanted to tell the nuzzling couple
that even if the dr gives them what they want,
there is no fixing anything.

stuffed bear on a left turn signal

make your dad some hair from your own

success and tell him you love him

i spun one strand out on espresso beans

and sewed a rupee into the countryside outside

Moscow. i couldn't decide

whether i wanted to stay there

in the glen of weeping where...where

do the stars go on vacation?

I stayed

for the spangled air clawing around the corner
of the ship side gate defrosting
as I waited for my boat to drop into ice,
eyes closed, wind lips as light as near dying
snow whipped across my forehead and, new goggles -

lost in the sea
before end of season.

I stayed
for the moments gone
as quickly as the letdown
of a single heartbeat,
the promise of polar bear
breathing in horizon,
the last droplet of water
to fall with August rain.

how papers sold

there i am, i proved to my son,

in the backwards curl of lowercase 'l'

scribbled loosely on the front page

of my cowhide notebook, a gift

i knew i'd receive as i cradled its pitted skin

in the abscess of my stepmother's shop.

there i am, i whisper

in the right loop of 'w'

claiming the blue leather folio -

an artifact from the artisan corridor

in Ushuaia, near the pier.

there i am, i croak

in the ink drag that means 'iff'

adopted after marriage and

before you, i told

my son, we learned

cursive on pages run

with triplet lines

shaped in the sound of the genuine

fever tree

i tell my son i need space
to sleep and ask him gently
to roll off my head every night,
around sunrise, i moan
at his darkened form curled around my neck
a plump hand for each side of my head and his nose
plugging my own as i whisper-beg *please baby,*
no ears. i roll away as the sparrows wake
and hours later as i wait under the first dried leaves falling
to retrieve him from school i think *what horrible*
woman turns from a clutching child.
does my coloring him in tender swirls of cloud
matter if his reaching eyes closed

and will he remember how many times
i say i love you, endlessly
as he falls asleep.

I don't listen for the old songs

anymore that start with it's terrible,

love; aren't you just terrified?

I don't listen for a diesel engine

pulling over salt water frozen

in pancake sheets that crackle

and buckle against the bow, my blood

eroding with every crashing note

of ice falling into Arctic Ocean.

I'm more scared now

of how easily the sun rises

of how hungry

I grow

for sunset, how little

I scream

against the wind,

dry with accepting

how complicatedly

caught

breath can breathe.

the catastrophe of after

my son asked which tree
an acorn grows into

and i realized i had no idea

whether i would transplant the dusty mason jar
of grandaddy's daddy's farm floor into michigan soil

where could i sow the yellow linoleum countertops, the heavy cut
glass casserole with marshmallows bubbling over the sides, all of the quilt

squares too close to the radiator glowing in hearty invitation, the man out
    back
rolling hay by hand into barrels i could never quite climb, an abandoned
    baseball diamond

grown over,

the shed with slim slate-tinted wooden slats rusted past the hinges and
    shelf
upon shelf of raspberry, strawberry, grape tomato preserves still warm
with grandaddy's daddy's fingerprints plus a smudge of tractor grease?
there weren't many books in the small white house by the highway.

i never sit on my front porch, but i did theirs, absorbing
dappled dusk pressed into the backsides
of rocking chairs swaying heavy
in north alabama early winter, late day,

the once-a-year snow flurry melting into untamed roadside.
my grandaddy's mama and daddy had craggy lidded eyes,
i reckon grandmama never wondered
how best to shadow them under the tight perm
she wore since grandaddy was born. she sewed her own

dresses and when there were too many children, she picked out
the stitches -
reshaped them into church shirts.
we sat on the fabric sofa
that felt like burlap and looked like my dad
's trousers in his bachelor-of-the-insurance-year magazine spread, 1982.
the smoky pattern would've belonged there
against a case of cigarettes,

i realized i had no idea
whether he ever got on
with my grandaddy.

the pillars of creation

you don't know who you are anymore

you're knee deep in adulthood with no concept

of what came before

the way to combat mental health crisis

5 incidents per memory, straight

in 5 neat lines

choose different types of life

experiences:

robotic

single

auto   pair,   new

life,   drop   in

never sure what qualifies

as an incident and don't forget

 to choose

 to stay.

if it could stay this heavy coal cloud morning

I'd find Amsterdam

behind my eyes, the Andaz,

with its blue fish head blue

on the wall behind

my bed

and a purple velvet hallway

in heavy drapes - everything grey, dark, grey

like damp linen on down daydreams

like palo santo billows in steam pressed sleep

crawling down an east Detroit sidestreet.

23:00 is chapped and gummy

between cheap flannel sheets

that'd probably catch fire

so I've set some constraints:

        r

     e g

   m   e

to not e

     o

to not r l

l   over,

to not

respond

  to the Winchester clock-chiming *bong,*

and the way my breath dropped

reminded me of the sound of blizzard

moving through Portal Point

into overturned kayak

a long way from Detroit,

where I know the frost flowers

are not like those in Tuscaloosa.

I believe everything lasts

longer in the cold, though
I've heard many of the oldest
people have survived in the tropics
or some awful flat in Alabama,
Iowa, or Pennsylvania
surviving

on soda and Marlboro's, maybe
I made that bit up

I used to tell myself
my lungs would recover
but now I'm not sure
I care or it matters
what's more

is wondering
whether I'll live beyond
the next election, if I have time
to tell my son I'll come
for him past policemen
holding other parents
I'll get through, I'll find you
what's more

is more
and more
years waiting

for a sea gull
far from sea flying
above the moon rise
over Michigan
and here
I am
howling

I slept in.
I drank cold water off New Jersey with small bits of ice, bleeding
into the waves as I drunkenly crawled along the salt flat full
with 4 pills in each hand meeting at the dance
up the beach and looking across the floor
toward my Mom who hadn't noticed

I'd gone
20 years ago

watching the show, realizing the woman
on the beach collecting bones
that seemed to come from birds
next to a bowhead whale rib –

this is how we prove the unprovable

showering off and using the thin two blade
razor under the sink for stray chin hairs

being held on a pale dock washed in late, late

late closing my eyes against all of the sweat
drying in cool snowflakes on tangled skin,
warm in how it read your body backwards

it was a long time
I wasn't there
a jack-in-the-pulpit
watching the maple
kestrel fall steeper
toward the rebound
of 10,000 years unlocked
in glacial melt and you
fingered the biological psychology
that hangs limp between sunset

and that blue curl of drawl lifting
the far left crease of your lips
as you breathe in a bit – *wait* –
with my salted hair alone
in you, in the *either* light

tomorrow or sunup,
which has always been
an unreliable narrator

have you ever reached
for something as delicate
as the last silk wing
disintegrating
on a sphinx
moth

the funny thing about dying tomorrow

is i want to touch all the paper i bled onto
and tongue the words breaking open against my teeth
like the first taste of pomegranate seed,
i told you how the ocean grows cold under frozen moon
and the surface tension seems to thicken
as i wondered, while floating past the break last week,

how still
i must be

to not upset the sea
and keep my nose above water

i told you i packed away
boxes of journals with different names on each,
so everyone gets a different narrative –

because when i die, tomorrow, it doesn't really matter
that i wanted the last line to taste
like a polar bear sliding along thin ice
to avoid collapse

the funnier thing about dying tomorrow

in november

the weeping ocean is still quiet
in undulation beyond the weeping beach

baldwin's nervous pills

fingers boil beneath surface tension
that just appears in gentle rolls
that furrow plowed into the sea
as if between crop rows
to collect the water
running

the funny thing about dying tomorrow
is remembering

my mom loved sassafras
at the top of the hill,
in autumn.

Carolyn Marie Rodgers said

if she couldn't use her brain
to write poetry, she didn't
want to be here. to be sure,
she didn't go

to the Cancer Institute of America.
and maybe i'd hide my cancer too,

for different reasons –

really, i guess, it was Carolyn's sister
who said all that about the no working brain, no new work
in an interview with *Poetry*, miles from Carolyn's revolutionary
writing period, her supposed dabble in spiritual lyricism - the 70s.
maybe I'd feel the same

about my work. maybe
without the poetry
i'm nothing
but a mess of tumors
lost in the radicalism of tender
normal. maybe
i am now, with it.

but let's be honest, as poetry
is meant to be, i'm nothing
like Carolyn Marie Rodgers
and never will be.

maybe

it'll be alright.

recovering

i can only see

light

dimly, as if walking alone

in a dark night cobblestoned

with gas streetlamps and stars

somewhere distant overhead

i want to find your heart

and bury it in my chest

once my eyes

are healed.

acknowledgements

canyon rain, Quagmire Magazine, December 2022

I believe everything lasts, Rising Phoenix Review, 2023

Emily is a writer and bookmaker living in Detroit. She's heavily guided by her work aboard expedition vessels as a naturalist in the polar regions, South Pacific and British Isles. Since retiring from shipboard life, Emily has focused on navigating her world as a woman, artist and mother. In 2022 she earned an MFA in Writing from the School of the Art Institute of Chicago, founded the MacGriff Writing Studio and joined the MA/MFA Design for Climate Action faculty at the College for Creative Studies.

www.ingramcontent.com/pod-product-compliance
Lightning Source LLC
Chambersburg PA
CBHW070453130626
46553CB00006B/2387